Recrowning God's Daughters II

An Anthology

TENITA C. JOHNSON

Published by So It Is Written, LLC
Detroit, MI
SoItIsWritten.net

Recrowning God's Daughters II: An Anthology

Edited by: So It Is Written – www.SoItIsWritten.net

Formatting: Ya Ya Ya Creative – YaYaYaCreative@gmail.com

ISBN: 979-8-9888204-6-8

LCCN: 2024903621

PRINTED AND BOUND IN THE UNITED STATES OF AMERICA

Table of Contents

Reclaiming My Crown

Kimberly Batchelor Davis

Tears streamed down my face and anger pulsed through my body while I hugged my knees. The sun was bright and high in the sky, and the stench of fish hung in the thick air combined with the pungent scent of tackle bait. The fishermen's voices rang loudly as they walked back and forth between the cabins and the pier. I sat on the bare wood floor in the summer cottage. I could hear my father and great-grandmother, Honey, yelling at each other. Several single-family white cabins sat nestled next to each other with the campgrounds off to the right and Lake Erie off to the left. Trailers of varying sizes dotted the campground with a huge open area for bonfires and barbecues. Lake Erie was bordered by a pier where the fishers sat and caught buckets of fish day in and day out. My bangs were puffy, scruffy, and they kept falling across my face. I swept my bangs away, although they would pop back into place like an old, worn rubber band. My long, thick dark brown hair had become swollen with the increase in humidity from Lake Erie although I tied it in a ponytail.

Muffled angry voices continued to pierce my ears, I looked up and saw my four-year-old baby brother come inside. The front screen door slammed. His yellow jersey and yellow short set were covered in sand. Tears welled up in his eyes. His short cropped curly hair was dotted with sand.

"Why is Daddy yelling at Honey?" my younger brother asked. "And why do I have to stop playing in the sand?"

"It's my fault," I cried. "Daddy is arguing with Honey because of me. I wanted to sit inside with her, and he said no. 'Children belong outside,' he said."

Tears bounced off of my cheeks, and I pulled my brother close to me and hugged him. He sobbed.

"You're okay," I promised.

This is one of the first times I remember taking off my crown. I relegated myself to a people-pleasing, neglectful, self-doubting version of myself.

Fast forward through my teen years into adulthood, and my people-pleasing, neglectful and self-doubting ways increased exponentially. These traits became the armor I wore and embraced without question. I believed in them. I lived by them, as if they were signature traits of my personal handbook. They became like weeds in the garden of my mind that would choke and suffocate me later on in life.

I allowed situations around me, which really had nothing to do with me, to affect me in negative ways that altered my personality. This practice continued on into the early days of my working life. I used to work with a lady who came to work daily with tales of woe and sorrow. My cube mates shook their heads at me because, each day, I listened to her intently and attempted to advise her. I counseled this depressed woman, who obviously had no one to talk to. I understood her pain. I believed because I knew what it felt like to not have anyone listen to me, I threw myself on the sacrificial altar. I vowed to be her listening ear and shoulder to cry on. Gwen, an elegant and graceful older woman with a salt and pepper bob and a thin athletic build, stopped me at the coffee station as I poured coffee into my orange mug.

"Hey, Kim! How's it going?"

I massaged my forehead as I closed my eyes and exhaled. "Whew," I said. "It's stressful. Reva came in and told me what happened yesterday."

Gwen drew her lip in and smiled. "Is that your problem?"

I cocked my head to the side. "Why do you say that?"

She reached over and placed her hand on my left shoulder and said, "Let her problems be hers."

"Kim, haven't you wondered why whenever she comes around, and starts sharing, we all walk away? You need to do the same. Don't let her steal your positive energy."

"You know I noticed that; however, I was always so focused on her."

Gwen stood up tall and straight like a spruce. "Right. Walk away. Don't entertain that foolishness," she said. "I don't mean her any harm, but sometimes people need to help themselves. She's an energy vampire."

I nodded. "Yeah. You're right. Every time I listen to her, I walk away exhausted."

That was a key ingredient in my people-pleasing ways. It only got worse as I got older. Opportunities poured in and, professionally, I grew. However, my people-pleasing, neglectful, and self-doubting ways continued on. I planned community outreach events and I learned to anticipate all of the problems that might occur. I lived with a negative mindset. I was always trying to stave off disaster, all the while neglecting myself. I would push through hunger, bathroom breaks, and long hours to make a project succeed. In reality, at my *real* job, I was making more money than my age. With real responsibility, I gained about twenty-five pounds. After my children, I gained another twenty-five pounds, which put my health in jeopardy with a type 2 diabetes diagnosis.

A healthy body and mind require adequate sleep, good nutrition, and exercise. However, I allowed other people's ideas of success and drive to motivate me instead of listening to what I needed and wanted. Again, I neglected my physical and mental needs for someone else's validation and applause. I was in competition with the world instead of myself. I lived by someone else's mantra, "Sleep when you're dead." The only motivation for me should have been *me*. However, I felt anxious if I was still or relaxed. Many people who I knew were doing amazing things, and I struggled to find myself. In constant motion, I was always trying to prove myself.

Envy filled me as I read about my friends who made the Thirty Under Thirty list by Crain's, the national publication, or the Forty Under Forty list. They were clearly leaders in their field. Although I was always overjoyed for my friends, there was always a tinge of sadness for me. When would people recognize that I was special? My self-doubting ways emerged, and they weighed me down in everything that I did. I always felt like I should be doing more, even when it was not necessary. I never, ever felt that I was good enough, and this was relayed to me in a conversation with a former boss. This conversation rings in my mind each and every time I have moments of self-doubt. Several years ago, I knocked on my boss' door and walked into her office. I sat down and received a valuable piece of advice.

"Hi, Voncile," I said. "What did you think of the event from this past Saturday?"

Voncile, dressed in an olive-green dress and blazer with short salt and pepper hair, leaned forward and said, "You know it went well."

I chuckled. "It would be nice to hear it from you."

Her face darkened. "You don't need to hear it from me," she said. "You need to believe that you did well. No one has to applaud you. Applaud yourself."

Upon hearing this, I felt immense frustration. All I wanted was for my boss to tell me that I did a good job. That I was valuable, worthy, and important. I needed to hear it. I craved it. Quite honestly, my self-esteem was in the toilet. Emotionally, I was overly sensitive and vulnerable. Yet, I always kept a wall up to protect myself. No one knew how I was really feeling—not even my husband. Unfortunately, the man who I thought was perfect proved to be human and capable of bringing disappointments and sadness to my life. It wasn't until later in life when a really good friend encouraged me to seek counseling and therapy that I realized how much anger, sadness, disappointment, and bitterness I held onto. And, yes, I was depressed.

Although, I was considered to have high-functioning depression, that simply means that I'm not the one who is so depressed that I'm unable to move. I could manage daily tasks and responsibilities; however, my patience was unusually short. I wasn't sleeping enough. I was eating poorly and not moving much at all to have influence in my weight. There were some moments when I would do better. Before my sons were born, I worked out daily and on the weekends with my friend, Gwen. We worked out at Powerhouse Gym and lifted weights for two hours each Saturday. The company that I worked for had a gym, and it was convenient to be able to exercise at work. Yes, I was a gym rat, with serious dedication. I had 180-185 pounds of muscle, and I was strong and healthy. Belly dancing and yoga were my other favorite extracurricular activities. My self-esteem improved and my self-worth grew exponentially. I had confidence; however, that all changed when I left the organization that I worked for and took on a higher position with more responsibility and more money.

A heavy-duty load, a lot of travel, and ever-increasing responsibilities left me reeling to balance my personal and professional life. My husband managed a basketball league that he founded, as well. Each Saturday, six hundred kids played through his program. Our schedules were polar opposite of each other. We were like two ships passing in the night. I excelled at work; however, I was failing at home. My husband and I never saw each other. Our close relationship began to fray. My issues with neglect and doubting myself resurfaced. I self-soothed with food and sabotaged all of the health benefits that I had cultivated. I made excuses that I was unable to work out due to my busy traveling schedule. My weight climbed and my self-esteem decreased. Work became my personal mission and validation, although when that began to unfurl, my self-esteem tanked even further.

The inner critic in my head recited more lies faithfully, as if it were the Pledge of Allegiance. Sadly, I listened. Pregnancy was unexpected for me. I was never the girl who dreamt of getting married or having children. I imagined myself traveling around the world, free and happy without a care in the world. After the birth of my second son, between sleep deprivation, general exhaustion and loneliness, post-partum depression set in. I was exhausted and I was infuriated. There was no family. I had no support system, nothing holding the tide of the pressures of parenthood back. I didn't have anyone to even offer a brief reprieve for a few minutes.

Desperately, I wanted to be *perceived* as a good mom. Inside, I felt like a failure and a fraud. I wasn't living. I didn't enjoy life. I was just barely getting through whatever came my way. My people-pleasing ways kicked into high gear once again. In my mind, it was a way to be included, loved and needed—no matter how much more I neglected and doubted myself. Things that once interested me were no longer important. I was knee-deep in questions and requests from people. It didn't matter if they were friends, co-workers, or an acquaintance. I would pull out my cape and wear it like I was Supergirl. In an instant, in a single bound and with a leap, I would whip out my phone and manage whatever problem needed to be overseen. This became such a habit that I never questioned if I could do it or even if I *should* do it. Later, I came to the realization that being accessible to anyone and everyone was sheer and utter exhaustion. During a trying time, in a feeble attempt to manage my mother's needs, my young sons, my fledgling business, and my own home, I broke down and cried at my dining room table.

"Why is it that I am always available for people, but when I need someone, no one is available for me?" I sobbed uncontrollably.

My husband wrapped his arms around me and sat down next to me.

"Because you're good at it," he said. "And you like to help people."

Anger rose in me, and I snapped. "We're supposed to help people if we're in a position to help."

Kevin, my husband, frowned. "I'm not saying don't help, but you don't know how to say no."

Later, I would understand what he said and why I needed to hear it. Oftentimes, I wished that my husband would have rescued me from my unhealthy habits and reassured me that, no matter what, I was valuable, loved and worthy. However, that never happened. I have since learned that fairy tales like what I desired are only written in storybooks. Therefore, I learned that if anyone was going to rescue me, it would be Jesus. I had to act. I couldn't wait for some imaginary prince charming.

I had to get the help that I needed. I had to make a conscious decision to heal from the pain and dismantle the lies about myself. There was no immediate fix. Nothing changed overnight. It was a long process that continues today. At my post-partum therapy appointment, I sobbed, snotted and cried uncontrollably. I was a bad mother and a horrible person because I didn't enjoy being a mom. The therapist let me ramble on for forty-five minutes and then he shocked me.

He said, "There's nothing wrong with you."

I looked at him wide-eyed and in disbelief. He spoke again. "You're tired. Exhausted."

I sniffed and thought, *This therapist must be off his rocker!*

He asked, "What do you do for yourself?"

I laughed. "Didn't I just explain to you all of the things that I had to do?"

He repeated. "You take care of your husband, your sons, your mom, your grandmother. Where are you on that list?"

I paused because I had no answer. Truth be told, I didn't believe that I deserved to be on that list. Why were my needs important when I was supposed to sacrifice my happiness for my children? I followed other people's perceptions. Oftentimes, people said, "It's all about the kids."

I believed that I didn't matter. My needs, desires and ambitions had to be abandoned. I was wrong on so many levels. This was born out of my husband and me parenting in a silo and me burying my feelings and thoughts. I struggled to believe that I was smart because I hadn't finished school. I wasn't accomplished. I hadn't received recognition or an award, although I have done some amazing things professionally and have since graduated. The conversation with my boss about being proud of myself rang in my ears. The anger was not there; only understanding of what that meant. Finally, fifteen years after that conversation, I finally got it.

My former boss wasn't insulting me. She was trying to prepare me not to look to anyone else for validation. I didn't understand that then. I get it now. Professionally, things have picked up for me again. I am once again in a semi-leadership role, doing outreach, which is what I excel at and love. The reality that depression will always be in my orbit, yet I have the power to break its control over me, sometimes brings sadness to me. I realize I have to work at keeping my mind and body in shape. Recently, I began a new nutrition and exercise transformation. Eleven pounds down and I not only feel better physically, but also mentally. The shackles of the past are a distant memory, with no willingness on my part to pick them up again.

Each and every day, it is a concerted effort that I must give to myself to eat well, pray, study my Bible, listen to the voice of the Holy Spirit, move my body and get as much restful sleep as my body needs. Some days, it's downright difficult because of my schedule and responsibilities. Yet, I'm worth every ounce of the struggle to care for me. My professional role is fraught with politics and differing visions. But, I'm a mom of a fifteen-year-old and a twelve-year-old, and I'm married. Studying the Word of God and listening to what He has to say about me has strengthened my resolve to be the best happiest version of myself. I keep Jeremiah 29:11 top of mind: *"For I know the plans I have for you," declares the LORD, "plans to prosper you and not to harm you, plans to give you hope and a future."*

This is my favorite Scripture. It brings peace to me when I'm struggling and when I need a quick word from the Lord. It also reminds me that God has made me a promise and the good things that I desire, He will bless me with them.

Psalm 37:4 says, *Take delight in the LORD, and he will give you the desires of your heart.*

Since, I've strengthened my relationship with Christ, there are many days when I know that God has carried me through. He's given me an utterance for an important project or program. He's encouraged me so that I could be of encouragement to someone else, even when I didn't feel like it. God has held my tongue, guarded my actions, and protected me from mishaps. None of this happened overnight. I cannot stress this enough. This is work and, no, it's not fair or easy. However, it is worthwhile. I'm worth it. I'm valuable. I'm loved. I'm important. I'm capable. And I matter, regardless of what anyone else has to say.

My only competition is *me* from the day before. No one else. I encourage you to *not* listen to the lies of the enemy. The inner critic in your head is simply that—the enemy spinning lies to you. Because you are going through a tough time, you listen and give space to the enemy to come in and take root in your mind. Take it from me. I have years of experience of feeding the weeds in my mind, which almost choked out the Word of God. Praise God for He is a conqueror! He has the victory. We are His followers. If we are obedient to Him and follow His precepts and His ways, we will be victorious, too. Victory is freedom from depression. It doesn't mean that I won't have future battles with depression. It means that, as long as I keep God first, depression will have no victory over me.

Philippians 4:6 says, *Do not be anxious about anything, but in every situation, by prayer and petition, with thanksgiving, present your requests to God.*

Pray. Study the Word and stay close to God. Nothing can separate you from the love of God. You may have problems, but they will not be able triumph over you. In Christ, we are victorious. You are victorious. Reclaim your crown in Christ and show them who you are. Show them who you belong to and be a light in a dark world. Remember that you are special, worthy, valuable and loved. You matter. May God bless you and keep you!

RECROWNING *& Reflection*

1. When did you begin to listen to the lies of the enemy, and why?

_____

_____

_____

_____

_____

2. What are the lies that you've been told or heard?

_____

_____

_____

_____

_____

3. What does God say about you? I challenge you to review the
   Scriptures that I used and see if they reveal the truth for you.

   _____

   _____

   _____

   _____

4. Who can you turn to to help uplift you, and who may need some
   encouragement from you?

   _____

   _____

   _____

   _____

5. What can you do to protect your mind and place your crown
   back on your head?

   _____

   _____

   _____

   _____

ABOUT THE AUTHOR

Kimberly Batchelor Davis

*K*imberly Batchelor Davis has been in love with books since she was a child. Who would've known that God would bless her with the gift of writing; however, he did, and she was reminded of that on September 11, 2001, after the devastating attacks on America. Kimberly's desire to write was renewed. Kimberly fervently believes that "We live by faith, not by sight" (2 Corinthians 5:7). It reminds us to continue to put our faith in God instead of ourselves. She realized that something was missing from her life; it was writing. She says: *"I had to have a purpose and it wasn't just about making money, I had to give back in some way—I just didn't know how."* Since then, she has not looked back. She provides a platform for the voiceless and by creating stories that have shared experiences which inspire or cause people to think about common experiences in a different way. Recently, she released two children's books "Rose and the Enchanted Seven" and "Look, Daddy! There's a Bunny. She has released "Escape to Paradise: Book 1, 2 and 3", the exciting, fictional romantic trilogy book series.

Kimberly is a contributing writer for *Date Night Magazine,* and she has been featured on the Brand-New Mommy and the Bougie Black Girl blogs where she discusses her bout of depression, motherhood and writing. She has published articles with Saved magazine and Mi Estilo, an online Hispanic magazine. She speaks professionally on issues that she's passionate about, which include motherhood, literacy, community civic engagement and writing. Kimberly has a Bachelor of Arts degree in Political Science from Wayne State University and is currently pursuing a Master of Creative Writing.

To contact Kimberly Batchelor Davis, please email knbdavis@gmail.com. You can also visit www.kimbdavis.com, www.twitter.com/batchelordavis, and www.facebook.com/batchelordavis.

The Missing Crown
Spiritual Lineage

Pearl Smith

After competing with women from all fifty states, women are judged on talent, health and fitness. After an evening gown, a private interview, and responses to an on-stage question, one fortunate woman would win the Miss America Pageant. Crowned by the year's previous winner, the winner receives flowers, solidifying her role as the next Miss America. With tears streaming down her face, she performs the iconic Miss America wave and thanks the nation for this honor. She is careful to hold the crown with one hand, ensuring it remains in its rightful place.

Having watched many Miss America pageants over the years, I have never once felt worthy of participating in such a beauty pageant, let alone winning a crown. I never felt deserving of love, much less a crown. A child deemed worthy is never rejected by a parent. I knew I was not worthy; I was rejected by my father from birth. He may have rejected me when my mom told him she was pregnant. However, I don't know that to be true because she never mentioned that to me.

My parents were teenagers when I was conceived. I do not know if they were in love or if they had a one-night stand that resulted in *me*. Understanding their story might help make sense of my existence. Even if I were the result of a traumatic event like rape, it could at least explain my father's absence. While such a circumstance might justify his decision to stay out of my life, I don't truly believe that was the case. Deep in my heart, I feel that each day, he consciously chose not to be a part of my life. For years, I waited for him to acknowledge me, to let me know that I was his child, and that I mattered.

I longed to be a priority for him. I yearned for him to whisk me away from the harrowing scenes of my mother enduring physical abuse at the hands of her many boyfriends. I often dreamed of sitting on my father's lap, resting my head against his chest and listening to the rhythm of his heartbeat. I imagined countless times how it would feel to be enveloped in his arms, receiving a gentle kiss on my forehead from my daddy. I wondered what affectionate nickname he might have for me. I thought his mere presence would have filled the void in my heart.

I wished he could have wiped aways my tears, the ones caused by the relentless teasing and bullying from my classmates and other kids in the neighborhood. As a young girl, I looked for my dad to rescue me. I waited for the day when his loving arm would wrap around me and assure me as only a father could. The deep-seated feelings of ugliness I harbored about myself might have healed if only he were there to tell me I was pretty—the prettiest girl he knew-- second only to my mom. But those dreams would never materialize. Instead, I was left to fend for myself, to find my own sources of encouragement, or to accept the harsh words of others and become what they labeled me. No one said I was royalty; therefore, for me, there was no reason to envision myself wearing a crown.

At the time, I did not know how to find my own encouragement. So, I internally embraced all the negative aspects of others' perception of me. Their negative perceptions held more weight than the positive perceptions. It appears no one appreciated a girl with nappy hair, a bald spot, and limited clothing who wore her school clothes twice a week because her mother couldn't afford new ones for her four children. I was born to a teenage mom. By the time I was in kindergarten, she already had four children. Today, she wouldn't even be old enough to buy an alcoholic beverage. With her limited education, she did her best to inspire us. But, as a high school dropout, she couldn't prepare me for growing up without a father. Despite her efforts to compensate for his absence, she could not take his place.

I remember a time in elementary school when I participated in a play about Rosa Parks. I was to play a little girl on the bus with her father. When it came time to say my line, I could not. I froze. The script required me to call a seven- year-old male classmate "daddy." I had never uttered those words before, and I certainly wasn't going to start uttering them with my classmate. My reluctance must have frustrated my teacher and classmates. My teacher tried her best to coax me into saying, "Daddy, what's going on?" She insisted that this was only a play. But, to me, it wasn't. It was real life. No one was going to take my father's place. With tears streaming down my face, I shouted, "He is not my daddy!" Even then, no one could take my father's place. No one would get the honor he should be getting from me. He was not my dad, and I could not give that honor to someone other than my father. I would not utter those words until I could say them to my real dad.

My father was a year older than my mom, but a teen father, nonetheless. I later found out that he was an alcoholic and addicted to drugs, marijuana, heroin and, finally, crack. Those were his drugs of choice. He was also addicted to women. His addictions were the priority in his life.

I have heard someone say, "You can't miss something you never had." This is confusing because I missed my father all the time.

In anguish, I lamented. I was the seed he planted. Why wasn't I worth watering? Like an unintended plant, I was left without any sunshine or water, slowly withering away, taking love or attention from anywhere so I could feel wanted, value, and needed. This led me to compromise many of the values my mother instilled in me. This also led to me leading a life of co-dependency, from buying gifts and giving my friends money, to giving myself to men I knew were not into me and accepting foul, disrespectful treatment. I would do anything to feel as though I mattered. I also struggled with insecurity. I compared myself to everyone based on whether I was good enough, pretty enough or worthy. I had a deep-seated depression that led me to walking the streets during the night while I should have been sleeping. This would be my life until December 1993.

Even as a young adult, my perception of myself was poor, ugly and unwanted. Why would I even be worthy of a crown? In fact, the very notion of me wearing a crown was alien to me. Beauty pageant winners, kings and queens don crowns as symbols of distinction and royal lineage. The crown serves a dual purpose. It distinguishes the ruler or winner, and it symbolizes their connection to the realm in which they govern. Their crowns are not just adornments, but legacies passed down. Kings' and queens' crowns connect them to their kingdom, their lineage and their past. But what crown could be passed on to a fatherless child like me? With no lineage to claim, my crown seemed like an impossibility. Instead of a regal bearing, I walked with the stoop of rejection, unaware of any royal ties.

I never realized that I, too, was part of a royal court. Oblivious to my own royalty, I wandered, not knowing that a kingdom was in some way, mine to accept and claim. Me, the fatherless child, the college drop-out, the single mother, a part of a royal lineage? Unbelievable.

When you don't know who you are, you are susceptible to anything. You wander around aimlessly. This is why it is important to know who you come from and whose kingdom you are a part of. God reminded me of the times when I would look out of my window as a youngster. I am not sure what I was hoping to see. Maybe Santa Claus in his sleigh or the moon turning to blood. These were things that I had heard about when I was a kid.

One time, while walking home from school, some girls from my class offered to walk with me. I was so excited to be included, until one of the girls jumped me. To this day, I am not sure why. In 10th grade, I ran for student council and won. I ran again in 11th grade. But during my speech, my classmates were laughing, and I lost the election. My hair was so short that my classmates called me "Baldilocks" (from the fairytale, *Goldilocks and the Three Bears*). Still today, I become insecure when people sit behind me, fearing they can see the invisible bald spot from my childhood. My hair has long since grown in.

The year 1993 was a pivotal year for me. I decided that I had had enough. At that time, I realized this fatherless daughter had spent all her time trying to convince people that she was worthy of love and acceptance.

On December 31, 1993, the man I was living with and dating at the time chose to spend New Year's Eve with another woman he had been seeing. Our relationship was a toxic mix of lies and infidelity, though over the past year, I had remained completely faithful to him. Despite feeling unworthy, I was exhausted from being taken for granted. I refused to accept this treatment any longer, regardless of my self-doubts. On that day, amidst my sense of worthlessness, I decided to stand up for myself. Since he chose to spend the night out, I packed all his things and put them on the front porch. I locked the doors so he wouldn't be able to get into the house. When he arrived, I simply let him know that he and I were no longer roommates and that he needed to find somewhere else to live. I feared being alone. I feared raising my children by myself. But I was even more afraid of what would happen to me if I did not love me enough to *choose me*.

Choosing me came with a lot of consequences and a hard reality I had to accept. I became a statistic. I was an uneducated, single mother on welfare, with two children out of wedlock with two different fathers. This was never my dream for my life, and it added to the insecurity I already felt about myself. I was supposed to go to college and become a doctor. I was not supposed to be intimate with anyone until I was married.

Throughout my life, I walked around without my crown. There were moments when I walked slowly into my royalty, but I had not quite grasped its value.

My life reminds me of Esther. Esther was a young Jewish girl when her parents passed away. As a young girl, I could not image what it would be like not to have either of your parents involved in your life. I imagine she could have felt lonely and insecure not having the support and guidance of her parents. Her uncle Mordecai took over the task of raising her. I wonder if she felt a void. I know I felt a void growing up without my father. I imagine an even greater void if I had not had either of my parents in my life. The Scriptures do not share if Esther allowed her circumstances to dictate her response to her life. But the Scriptures do say there is nothing new under the sun. Her circumstances prepared her for what God had in store for her. I am sure Esther cried at night, thinking about her parents. I know that she longed for their presence. My mom did not take the place of my father not being there. Mordecai could not take the place of her parents not being there.

The king at the time was Xerxes. Xerxes was in the market, looking for another queen to replace Vashti, who was the previous queen. Mordecai recommended Esther. Esther was sent to live at the palace to prepare to be chosen as queen. Each woman went through a combination of rituals and purification sessions to prepare for becoming queen. Esther's preparation included a combination of physical, intellectual and spiritual elements. It took courage, faith and the importance of wise counsel, which she would use in her role as queen. These sessions went on for months before the queen was chosen. Once the preparation sessions were over, the queen was chosen, and a crown was placed on her head.

The king found delight in Esther and chose her to be his queen. She was chosen. From being an orphan and being raised by her uncle, to living in the kingdom without her only family and being purified to being trained to be a queen, Mordecai helped Esther understand who she was. I believe, at first, she was uncertain of her role. There are times when other people can see who you are before you see it yourself. Once Esther understood her role and what her crown meant, she used her royalty to save her people. There was a plan and a purpose for her struggle. If everything had gone the way she would have desired, she would not have been in the palace for such a time as this— the saving of her people.

As I look back on my life, I am grateful for the lot I was given: the lot of being a fatherless daughter. While I longed for my father's presence in my life, I now understand that my life would have been different had he been a part of it. I imagine being a part of a drug-infested culture. My father was addicted to drugs since his teenage years. My mother never wanted to be a part of that culture. He was in and out of jail for various illegal activities. My father was uneducated and never really held a job—outside of the job his stepfather provided for him when he was not in jail or running the streets. I never had to worry about drug raids, physical abuse, things being stolen from our home and sold for drugs, not having food to eat because there was no money to buy food, or a mom who succumbed to a dad's urging to become a part of the drug culture. None of those things became my reality.

While I met my father in person when I was twelve years old, I got to know him when I was in my mid-30s. He was clean at this time and stayed clean until his demise. He later walked me down the aisle at my wedding. He became a real grandfather to my youngest child. He loved my husband. He finally treated me as his daughter, dying less than five years after I got to know him. I could have felt cheated, but I didn't.

The only way I was able to embrace my father and accept him for who he was, was to see him through the eyes of my Heavenly Father. He was my Heavenly Father's son, as well. He was the earthly man that my Heavenly Father chose for me. I also learned to embrace my Heavenly Father. I used to feel alone. But when I look back at my life, I see all the ways my Heavenly Father protected me.

He allowed my father to walk away from me so that I would not be caught up in a drug-infested lifestyle. Even though my mother was being physically abused by her boyfriends, He allowed her to gain courage, to take her crown back, and to walk away from those relationships. She is my hero. Even though I had children out of wedlock, and I dropped out of my undergraduate studies to raise my children as a single parent, my Heavenly Father allowed me to keep my dreams. Eventually, I returned to school, completing my undergraduate degree, an MBA, and pretty soon, a doctoral degree. My daughter is in nursing school. My son graduated from Eastern Michigan University, and my third child will be graduating from high school soon. I have held several management positions, led a few Bible discussion groups and authored a few books. But my greatest achievement was embracing my place in God's (my Father's) royal kingdom.

It was the moment when I gained the courage and the conviction to take my crown back, embrace my royalty, and wear my crown. Early that year, as I was lying on my bed, I vividly heard the voice of God telling me that He wanted me to follow Him. It would take almost the whole year before I surrendered and understood what He was calling me to. My missing crown was found. I put my crown on and walked away from what held me back from my destiny.

In December of 1993, when I made the decision to no longer hold on to the things that held me hostage and walk away from those people who were holding me hostage, I was able to see myself differently. I was able to step out on faith and choose to do things my Heavenly Father's way. I always had a Father who was there. I was *wanted*. I was a part of a royal priesthood. I was *chosen*. I belong to a holy people. Someone like that *should* wear a crown.

So, each day, I put on my crown with confidence, knowing I was chosen to wear it. I am not bothered by what others think of me because my Father thinks of me with high regard, and He is the one who spurs me along.

RECROWNING *& Reflection*

1. What pivotal moment in your life shaped your thoughts about your value?

_____

_____

_____

_____

_____

2. How was your earthly father instrumental in shaping your view of yourself? Your view of God?

_____

_____

_____

_____

_____

3. The Scriptures say that God is a father to the fatherless. When looking at God as a father, can you look back in your life and see where God showed up as a father would?

_____

_____

_____

_____

4. God says that you are a part of a royal priesthood. Knowing this is your lineage, how does this change your view about you and your life?

_____

_____

_____

_____

5. Esther was both fatherless and motherless. Describe the void she may have felt without her parents. What about when she was being purified and, during that time, she did not have any family members there to support her?

_____

_____

_____

_____

6. What would you have to change to embrace your lineage and wear your crown with confidence in its purpose?

_____

_____

_____

_____

_____

7. We are born into royalty. Yet, we don't always know or embrace this status. What are some of the ways in which you looked for your worth elsewhere, when you should have been looking toward God's kingdom?

_____

_____

_____

_____

_____

ABOUT THE AUTHOR

Pearl Smith

$\mathcal{W}$hile many people choose to march to the beat of their own drum, she understands that, without the support of others, that beat is incomplete. For Pearline Smith, author and motivational speaker, her passion for helping women see themselves as God sees them—and fully become that woman—makes her a magnet for those who need help, hope and healing. Affectionately known by many as simply Pearl, her pearls of wisdom and knowledge usher others into a life of fulfillment and wholeness—allowing them to become the gem they were originally intended to be.

As a great observer, keen listener and encourager, many people mistake this "quiet storm's" meekness for weakness. However, it's anything but. As a healthcare worker by trade, her innate ability to care for others, coupled with her passionate patience, positions her as a highly sought-after professional across multiple industries. A creative storyteller in her own right, Pearl is intentional about not just meeting new people, but learning more about their personal journey. From failures and successes to disappointments and dreams, she speaks to everyone she encounters right at the point of their need—reassuring them that God has not left them and that He has a greater plan at work than what meets the eye.

Holding both a Bachelor of Science in Health Administration and an MBA, Pearl argues that no matter how much we have obtained alone, we are so much more alike than we are different. While many women fight and belittle their way to the top, she argues that instead of envying each other's success, women could go much further together than they can alone. Whether it's through her literary masterpieces, or her speaking engagements at conferences, her message is the same: We ascend higher faster when we collaborate, not compete.

Having published her first book, *Walking to the Beat of My Own Voice in 2018*, Pearl continues to empower women through her messages of triumph after tragedy. Contributing author of *From Fatherless to Fearless II*, Pearl is committed to letting women know she understands their struggles of not having an earthly father's validation. She strives to encourage women to know and to embrace their Heavenly Father who validation unconditional. Whether you've encountered her one time, or too many times to count, Pearl leaves a mark on the hearts and minds of others that cannot easily be erased—inspiring them to be the best version of themselves and to see the best in others.

For more information or booking, email pearldickerson@yahoo.com or call 248.514.3165.

The Hijacked Crown

Barbara A. Foster

I grew up in a single-parent home that included myself and three siblings. I didn't have a father in the home. My mother sometimes worked odd jobs or went to foodbanks just to make ends meet. Even still, there was great lack in the home. I was around the age of nine or ten years old when my sister asked my little brother and me to accompany her to the corner market, as she had done so many times before. As we entered the market, my sister proceeded to go into the meat department. She went near the ground beef and, surprisingly, proceeded to put the meat in her pants. Once the meat was concealed, she urged my brother and me to walk fast behind her. As we got closer to the door, I could hear the pounding of enormous footsteps.

A loud voice yelled out, "Hey! Come back here with that meat!"

My sister proceeded to tell my brother and I to run. We ran quickly away from the market and stopped once we reached a safe distance, which was a few houses from home. This may seem troublesome for some. But for my siblings and me, it was a day that we didn't have to make pancakes with flour and water or eat boiled eggs. This is, by no means, a jab at my mother. She was doing the best she could as a single mother. Not to mention that she was not aware of what took place that day.

I felt a great sense of poverty when we stole from that market, as I had felt many times before.

As I matured, the way I viewed money was tied to how I view myself and my self-worth.

I saw money as power, respect and acceptance. It was a license to do anything, say anything, and no one would question or correct you. I watched people in my family who were financially stable talk to and treat folks as if they were nothing. No one ever corrected them or said anything. All of the negative comments were greeted with a, "I might need your help one day!" followed by agreeing smiles and the nodding of heads. But once they were out of the presence of that family member, people huddled and spoke about how terrible that person was after making their belittling comments.

Not having enough finances made me feel unvalued. I was not worthy to speak up and I did not feel accepted.

Not having the basic things or finances created a since of inadequacy, unworthiness and low self-esteem the more I compared myself to my peers, the more I felt hopelessness. For instance, when I began building a relationship with my father and my two siblings who were raised by my father, I compared their accomplishments to what I have or haven't accomplished. But I had to remind myself that we had two different set of circumstances. The biggest difference is that they had the support of a father present in the home. In my opinion, that's why they were able to achieve their goals.

I didn't feel important until around my early twenties when I began to tie material things to how I viewed myself. I would sell, buy or steal if I had to. It was almost like a drug. It wasn't that selling my body or stealing that was like a drug. It was the acceptance that I got from others that was like a drug. It was very intoxicating. But, just like a drug, the high only felt good in the moment. The moments were so short-lived.

I got so lost in the way, I eagerly wanted people to see me, that I lost my own self-respect, and I compromised my dignity.

It was also the way I wanted others to view me. It wasn't until the end of 2019 that I felt optimistic about my financial status. Some might consider what I had as little to nothing, but it was everything to me. I had never been in a place financially where I was able to say that, "If I left my job or was terminated, I could live for a decent amount of time off what I had saved." I got my credit score into the "excellent" status. That was amazing to me, coming from the poor and even poor rankings.

I met some people through a friend whom I pretty much trusted like a relative. They were supposed to be investing my money to help make me more money. That was the promise. I was hopeful. I was optimistic. I was excited to double, if not triple, my investment. Little did I know what I'd gotten myself into.

The *first* time (yes, this happened more than once), these investors asked me for $10,000. I didn't really have to do anything besides invest. The money was going to multiply on its own. As it accumulated, these people simply made a percentage off of the profit of the investment. Even though I had not yielded a return on the initial investment yet, they soon asked me if I wanted to make another investment. Not expecting anything out of the normal, I invested another $5,000.

When I asked about how my investment was doing, they simply said, "You haven't lost anything. You have to be patient. It takes time. Even though it might dip a little bit that doesn't mean that you're losing out. That's just how the market goes. It goes up and down. But stay faithful."

By the time I invested in the second stock, they told me, "If you want to go ahead and invest in that one, you'll probably get a quicker return off of that investment than the first one because it's less money and less people are buying into it."

I wasn't focused. All I was thinking about was getting extra financial help because I needed it. With the way my situation was set up, not to mention my son and I had just relocated, so we needed a cushion. I didn't know how long it was going to take me to find a new job in a new state.

Many people called me crazy, but I left Michigan and moved to South Carolina. I didn't know anybody there. But I was obeying the voice of God. I went, even though folks were indirectly and directly telling me not to go. I was still working virtually for my job in Michigan while I was in South Carolina. I resided in both states at the time. But the goal was to invest the money and flip it to earn more money to help me get out of debt. I also wanted to get ahead and purchase a home in South Carolina.

I didn't do my due diligence. I didn't Google the company or check the people out online to make sure they were legit. During that time, not only had my nephew passed away, but I was dealing with adjusting to moving to another state. All of that took a toll on me. When my nephew passed away, I went through extreme depression. Anybody could have walked up to me and told me to do something, and I would have done it. My mental state was severely weak. I was vulnerable. I was barely making it through the day.

After I invested the $5,000, I didn't hear from the investors anymore.

I called repeatedly. I called for a week straight. Then, I stopped calling for a few days. When I called back, the phone went straight to voicemail. That's when I realized what this really was and everything it was not.

They'd swindled me out of my money.

They just ran off with my money.

I was so engulfed with emotional pain that I couldn't even really think about the money. I was dealing with so much depression and anxiety that the money was not my focus. I was focused on trying to live. I was trying to stay alive— literally, spiritually and physically.

I cried for a few days. I couldn't believe God had let this happen to me. I trust others easily. Sometimes, to a fault. I didn't pray. I didn't seek God. I didn't phone a friend to ask for their opinion.

I was ashamed to tell anyone. I thought to myself, *You're so stupid! You so dumb! You met these first set of people and they took your money. Why would you give your money to somebody else? Why would you do that? What is wrong with you?*

At that moment, I questioned everything God had ever spoken to me, including the decision to transition from one state to another. Everything was in question at this point.

I asked myself, "How could a full-grown adult still make decisions like this?" I felt incompetent. I didn't feel capable of making any decisions. At that point, I thought that maybe, just maybe, everything everyone has ever said negatively about me since I was little was true. Maybe I *was* slow. Maybe I *was* dumb. Maybe I *was* stupid. Every negative word or thought came crashing down on me.

The thoughts got so intrusive and painful to the point that I contemplated taking my life. At the same time, I didn't want to die. But how could I live past this feeling of failure? I felt as if I had nothing to live for. But what I realize is that I didn't think about the loss of money more than how I would appear in the face of people who I wanted to accept me. Yes, I grieved the money like it was a death. I went through every stage of grief. I didn't believe this was happening. Then, I questioned why this was happening. I started bargaining with God. I promised God that I would do everything He told me to do from that day forward if He'd simply fix this and take the pain away. In my moments of depression, it was too much to bear. I just wanted to die.

I laid in bed for three weeks with no food or shower, contemplating how I would take my life. Every morning that I woke up, I would curse at God for waking me up.

Just like the loss of a person, the loss of money came with much grief. I had to take time to process what had just happened to me and how I missed all the signs. I still had to keep trying my best to keep moving forward. I went back to see my therapist. I knew I had to start seeing him again if I was going to continue living. Even seeing him didn't seem like it was really helping. The depression got worse. I told my doctor I needed medication. But the medication only caused me to sleep more every day. But, somehow, it kept me alive.

I kept hearing the Holy Spirit tell me, "If you can make it through this, you will never have to do this again."

I kept looking at my age. At the time, I was forty-eight years old. I was completely embarrassed to even tell anybody about what happened. I felt stupid. I felt like the stupidest person that God created. I asked myself over and over again, "Why didn't I hear from God concerning those people who took my money?" The answer was that I didn't seek Him for guidance because I allowed my emotions to determine my direction. Then came the intrusive feelings of worthlessness. The feeling of low self-worth made me feel as if I wasn't worthy of dating or marriage. I didn't deserve to go anywhere. I didn't need to go outside. I didn't need to do anything. The way I viewed myself was horrible.

I feel like I aborted the mission in South Carolina. I feel like I left before I was supposed to leave. My stepfather almost passed away and the pain I heard from my mother traumatized me. I knew my mother wanted me to come back.

When I came back to Detroit, it was really rough. I beat up on myself a lot. I felt like such a loser. I was concerned about what people were thinking. Coming back to Detroit and having to face the naysayers was beyond challenging. It took me a minute to get to the point where I didn't care what others thought. But I got there.

I'm slowly but surely coming out of the weeds, where I'm able to think clearly. I'm putting value in myself again. I'm worthy of dating somebody. Today, I can enjoy jobs, friendships and romantic relationships. God continues to surround me with people who pull me up and out.

One of the directors at my job said, "You're not the only person that this has happened to at this age. You're going to be okay. It's all right."

The Holy Spirit told me, "You got to stop comparing yourself to what you feel like you want people to see you as. Everybody makes mistakes. Everybody makes bad decisions. Some people's bad decision- making is bigger than yours."

This was a clean slate. I had to get up. I had to figure this thing out. I had to put something in motion. I had to find the money. I found the money to invest in another business. But, this time, I was in control of what was going on. I invested in a franchise. I wasn't relying on anybody to do the work for me.

In the midst of all I went through, not only did they steal my money. They hijacked my identity. They hijacked my self-value and self-worth. I lost so much in the process that I felt like nothing, and I felt like I had nothing. It was an expensive lesson to learn, but I learned indeed the hard way. Don't let anybody pressure you into deciding before you're ready to decide. If I have to give you an answer right now, the answer is, "No." If I can't have time to pray on it, if I don't have seven days, the answer is, "No." Remember that, "No," is a complete sentence and it doesn't require further explanation.

Also remember that God is in the midst of chaos, too. He knows what's going on. Nothing surprises Him. He's right there to pick up the pieces when we get off track. He promised to never leave us or forsake us. Trust God. Even though this was a hard place to be in, I still wouldn't change it. I wouldn't change none of it. The Bible says that all things work together for our good. In the midst of my poor decision making, He can still make it work together for my good.

Today, my mind is stronger. I'm still working. I'm still rebuilding. I feel like the smoke is clearing. I actually get up in the morning with a plan. Sometimes, we can forget that we have a crown. We have to continually remind ourselves that it's there. Sometimes, it may need to be readjusted from being knocked around and even knocked off due to the cares of this life. As I wrote this story, I wondered, *How can I help someone when life is still life-ing on me?* At the same time, I sit here and am grateful because I lived to tell the story and it didn't kill me mentally, spiritually or emotionally, although the ultimate plan was for my assassination.

Part of my recovery process was regaining my peace. I needed to recover and rebuild from that loss. I decided liquidating my debt was the best option. I needed a clean slate, a fresh start, if I must say. And this was the way up and out. I'm still silencing the voices that are in my head that sometimes show up in my own voice or the voices of others, that say, *"How could you have fallen for something like that? That would never have happened to me! Girl, don't tell anyone else about what happened because that was just dumb."* But God saw fit to point me to the Word, which tells me that all things work together for the good of those who love Him and who are called according to His purpose. I now do my research on any and every business venture that I'm considering. I'm in the process of starting a janitorial service, but I'm moving with caution. I'm not allowing fear to cripple me from making more investments.

But God had to point me to the Word to remind me that He did send me to South Carolina, just like he told Abram to leave his native country, his relatives, and his father's family, and go the land that He would show him.

I wish that I was as obedient as Abraham so that I could have seen what the end of the thing was going to be. But fear got me. That's okay. I still learned my lesson. Getting to the place of peace and acceptance is still sometimes challenging. However, I am light years away from where I started from.

RECROWNING *& Reflection*

1. When have you had to rebuild and how long did it take?

_____

_____

_____

_____

_____

2. What has been your greatest fear about starting over?

_____

_____

_____

_____

_____

3. How can God get the glory out of those times we are swindled
    or tricked?

    _____

    _____

    _____

    _____

    _____

4. Do you tie your financial status to your self-worth? If so, what
    are some ways to change that?

    _____

    _____

    _____

    _____

    _____

ABOUT THE AUTHOR

Barbara A. Foster

*C*ommitted to helping people within her community find resources through volunteering and direct action, Barbara A. Foster has been working with people experiencing homelessness for over 20 years. She also has massive experience planning events to assist those suffering from food insecurities. When she's not serving within her community and within her church, she enjoys spending time with her children and grandchild, who are her reasons for everything. She strategically aims to encourage those who feel like they can't make it when the going gets tough. Her passion is people, and she expresses that passion by serving through words of encouragement, empowerment and support.

The Refined Crown

Dr. Teresa Moore

" *I* am *sicka* this! *And*, I am sick of people abusing and misusing me, my love, and my loyalty. Taking my kindness for weakness. It never fails; I always find myself here! Every time I extend myself to others, I am the one left hurt, broken and feeling misused. I mean ... really God? How many times will my heart be shattered, crumbled, and handed back to me? The abuse, disrespect and hurt I endured has been an ongoing cycle for as long as I can remember. Most of this anguish I experienced was caused by those who proclaimed to love me, and those I loved. Funny thing is, I thought love was not supposed to hurt..."

During this time in my life, I was living aloud 1 Corinthians 13:4: *"Love suffers long and is kind."* Suffering was like a safety blanket that I never asked to have.

During the 70s and 80s, my momma was out doing her thang and Papa was a rolling stone, to say the least. So, my early years were spent with my godparents, until Papi died, and Bae Bae moved to California. By this time, I was in junior high school. My momma had a crib in the projects. Living with my momma was not easy, especially since I was angry that she left me while she ran the streets. Not to mention I felt abandoned by Bae Bae because she left me to go live in California with her family. Man, I just could not escape folks leaving me! Now I was focusing on how to survive in the projects with a mother who had no money. At least when I lived with my godparents, I ate every day, I was clean, and I was safe most of the time. Things changed! I spent many days alone, hungry. I was trying to maintain my sanity. While most children were living a foot-loose and fancy-free life, I was forced into a survival-mode lifestyle.

Growing up in a poverty-stricken area without my siblings and a present mother, all I really had was my homegirls. At the time, it was enough for me. God blessed me with a cousin my age and two besties. We quickly became four-the-hard way. Out of the four of us, I was the one in the bunch who experienced lack the most. My two besties and my cousin were living better than I was, and they looked out for me and made up for what I lacked. God had truly blessed me during one of the most challenging times of my life, and I was thankful for Him.

Before meeting my two homegirls, I had my cousin. However, she did not live within walking distance. So, I only saw her at school. Being alone at such an early age really took a toll on me. But, as I look back, it was in those moments that God's Word became alive right before my eyes. Hebrews 13:5 was at work in my life, and God's promise to never leave me nor forsake me was manifested. At the time, I was unaware because I did not know the Word of God. I was used to people disappointing and abandoning me. God was always with me, and He promised to remain with me, even until the end of the world.

Having little knowledge of God's presence, coupled with the fact that I can't see Him, I craved the essence of physical touch. So, having my homegirls helped fill the lonely void. For the first time in my life, I had sister-friends. Friendships were, and have always been, significantly important to me. In my mind, nothing was greater than the bond I shared with these three. I trusted them. They brought happiness and security into my life. Most of all, I felt safe when I was with them. I could share my heart's desires, my fears, and disappointments with them. Each of them added a level of joy to my life. We made plans of what our lives would look like, and we planned to be besties forever. We spent hours on top of hours making plans for our futures. Hours of laughing, eating, doing each other's nails, and talking aimlessly on the phone until one of us fell asleep was the norm. We were joined at the hip. You did not see one of us without the other two— until the unimaginable happened.

I started dating my daughter's father when we were in our early teens. He was this outspoken, rebellious man who grabbed my attention with his boldness. We quickly became inseparable; he was the first male that *semi-kept* his word to me. He was also the one who introduced me to the dope game. Whew! My life at that time changed for the better. I was no longer in lack, and I was in love. I was on the come up! I was driving cars, wearing new clothes and sporting gold chains. My attitude elevated ten degrees. I had come a long way from not having any food, not being able to pay my momma's bills, and barely making ends meet. I was living the life! I had a boyfriend. I had my girls and a few dollars. And my momma came back home. Life was good.

Good things were happening with me and my homegirls. My besties and cousin were dating, too. But, as fate would have it, I became pregnant. I was sixteen years old at the time and, according to my momma, keeping my baby was not an option, even up to the six- month point. Despite the devastation I experienced, my girls were right there to help me get through that painful moment.

I became pregnant again two years later.

This time, I was determined to keep my baby. This is when things changed. I no longer had two besties. The circle was reduced to one and my cousin. One of my besties, my ride-or-die, my secret-keeper, crossed an unrepairable line. She slept with my daughter's father. The wind was knocked completely out of me. I could not breathe.

How could she do this to me? She was supposed to be my daughter's godmother. She was going to be an honorary TT and the dependable babysitter. That moment shaped the way I viewed every other relationship I would encounter. I was hurt by my boyfriend and my bestie, and I vowed to never let people get close to me again. This situation destroyed our bond and neither of us were ever the same. I had trust issues. And, once again, I was abandoned by two people whom I loved.

Several years after the betrayal of my daughter's father and bestie, I continued to live a guarded lifestyle—until I *really* gave my life to Christ. Prior to that devastation, I had never had a real encounter with God. In fact, attending church was haphazard when I was younger. That all changed on April 27, 1997. This was a moment in time that I will never forget. It was just one week after my first wedding anniversary. I walked into this beautiful building and was greeted by several people before taking a seat. The choir was amazing, but the preached Word was life changing. It was as if God Himself was talking to me. I eagerly made my way to the altar once the invitation for salvation was given, and I have not regretted that decision.

Being born to a crack-addicted mother, I had no real example of what a loving family looked like as a young child. So, to have a church family who loved me was the best gift God could have given to me. I am reminded of the story of Hagar in Genesis 16 *when she proclaims him to be El-Roi, the God who sees her.* God had once again supplied my need! I finally had a family. I was excited and scared all at the same time. He saw *me!*

Accepting Christ was one of the best decisions that I could have ever made in my life. Yet, it did not come without a price tag. I lost some stuff! Acquaintances switched up on me. Some family turned away from me. Life as I knew it would soon change. Folks were leaving rapidly. This time, people left me because I wanted to really get to know Jesus. I talked about Him. I read the Bible. I earnestly wanted a changed lifestyle. Unfortunately, this agitated some when I turned away from worldly things. My home was no longer a weed house. There were no more midnight smoke outs, dice games and Sega Genesis game matches. I was not judging them for their lifestyles; I just knew mine needed to change for the better. Losing acquaintances and having family change up on me left me devastated and feeling alone. *Again!* The embrace and encouragement I desired never happened from the ones I thought should have given it to me. To my surprise, I was well received and welcomed by my new church family. This was new to me. I wasn't sure how to receive love from strangers.

I was thankful for the love. I'd wanted for so long for someone to love me, to see me, and to know that I mattered. Prior to joining church, I struggled daily with rejection. My days were filled with reminding myself that I was no longer the crack-addicted little girl anymore. I did not have to be afraid to trust again. I had to remind myself that everyone is not out to hurt me. I had a church family who loved me and now all my problems would disappear ... or so I thought.

Immediately, I started serving in my church. Whatever my hands found to do, I did! I was happy to serve. However, what I did not know was that everyone attending church was not saved. Many of them had just as many issues as me. I had a rude awakening! When I joined church, I was all in. I thought all the other members were, too! I did not know any other way to be. So, to my surprise, when I experienced my first hurt in the church, I resorted back to what was familiar. The little girl, abandoned, went to sit in the corner! *Friendless.* Now, I was angry as I pictured her slouched down in a corner, crying and afraid, simply wanting her mommy. I can feel myself reaching out for her, grasping the air, only to be confronted with the fact that she is not coming. *But where is she? Why isn't she here to help me? Mommy!*

Mommy! Where are you? I was abandoned by my mother, my best friend, my daughter's father, and now, church folk!

Forming friendships became easy at my new church. So, it was no surprise when I developed a relationship with some new sisters. Things were going well in the beginning, but soon, I noticed a change. It became increasingly hard to be around one of them. It seemed as though, when I had encounters with her, she was always confrontational. Eventually, she stopped speaking to me. I was unaware if I had offended her. So, I tried to apologize to no avail. Nothing that I tried changed her demeanor toward me. I stopped trying. There I was again, left by someone I loved, not knowing what I had done to make her turn away from me.

I began to see some of the characteristics of my mother, bestie, and daughters' father present in the people I served with in church. Oh boy! I thought to myself, *This cannot be happening! Not with my beloved church sister.* This time around, I did not run away! This was my church, and I made up my mind that I was staying. For many years, I ran away from rejection. But not this time. I loved my church, and I was determined to stay. I chose to serve with the saints. Although that particular relationship was severed, there were many that were not. However, my guard was back up. I was having a tough time trusting those I served with in ministry, to say the least.

There were several incidents that took place, and I knew I had to deal with my emotional "stuff"! This was the beginning of my therapy and healing journey. I learned that I was being refined and that God's process would make me complete. During this process, I looked at me. What I saw looking back was a work in progress. I acknowledged that my being abandoned and rejected as a child helped to shape my character and my love language. I have a need to give to others physically, mentally, and emotionally because that is what I needed. I have spent years trying to be to others what I needed my mother, father, and friends to be to me. This is why it hurts. *I am not either of them!* I often reminded myself to pause. I knew I had to put in the work. I am no longer in that place. So, why do I allow the enemy to take me back to what used to be comfortable?

I am used to showing up 100 percent for every person I am connected with because I do not want anyone to experience abandonment. This can be a blessing and a burden. I rarely get a fraction of what I give out. In return, I am left empty. This happens more often than I care to discuss. The enemy used those times to torment me. Before long, I partnered with him and threw a pity party. God began to show Himself to me and all the ways that He has remained faithful and present in my life. He also reminded me of what Satan's job was to do to me. More importantly, He told me in in Isaiah 43:1 that I belonged to Him. This revelation removed the scales from my eyes. God was refining me, and I no longer wore abandonment like a blanket. God loved me, even when others walked away. He was the constant in my life. I spoke back to the enemy for we are not friends. I stopped playing that song and dance with him! He is a liar and the father of lies. According to James 4:7, resisting the enemy will cause him to flee from me. Furthermore, 2 Corinthians 2:11 reminds us that God would not have us be ignorant to the devices of Satan.

The refining process was difficult. God was removing the seeds that the enemy had planted in my mind, heart, and life. These seeds had caused me to, not only feel abandoned, but to live as such. During the refining process, the Lord breathed upon my talents and giftings. That's when the real problems started. The more my light shined, the more things I became involved in. Some were God-ordained; some were just people using me for my talent. During this time, I was convinced that God was using me for His glory. Boy, was I wrong. Being busy does not equate to being productive. In most cases, I was just busy. God was not getting any glory. I was people-pleasing, not pleasing God.

While in the refining process, I noticed a few things happening within me: growth, pruning and restoration. As my relationship grew with the Lord, when uncomfortable situations arose, I no longer responded the same. Instead of resorting back to a familiar place of listening to the lies of the enemy, I used tools learned in therapy. I paused, prayed and faced the journey head-on, knowing Jesus had my back.

Jesus and counseling should be mandatory for every believer. Both were, and still are, the answers and solution to every problem. I allowed the Lord to work on me! I literally put myself in time-out and feasted on the Word of God. I asked the Lord to let the Word become flesh inside of me so I could live as His daughter. For I knew that He was my Father. Wherever I made my bed, He would be there. I had been joined to His family, and abandonment would never be a part of our relationship.

The pruning in the refining process almost took me out! I dealt with self-esteem issues for so long that I had to be taught that I was enough. During the lesson, I learned that I was royalty. I no longer had to live as though I was *not*. I learned to give myself permission to be free from needing validation from others. God is my validator. Through His Word, I challenged all negative thoughts and replaced them with His promises.

Restoration and healing went hand in hand during the refinement process. I spent many hours on the altar, allowing God to alter me. God altered my heart, and I forgave all those who abandoned and left me. Forgiveness really is an intoxicating fragrance that is pleasant to God. It is also a requirement from Matthew 6:15: *"But if you do not forgive others, then your heavenly father will not forgive your trespasses."* God restored the relationships with me and my parents. My mother and I eventually developed a loving relationship. Sadly, the relationship with the bestie who slept with my daughter's father was not repaired; however, I forgave her. Healing is a daily journey. As we go, we will grow. Even though all of the relationships were not restored, God more than made up for them. There is nothing in our lives that is removed that God does not have the power to restore even greater.

Being in a place of continual refining, God has replaced every friend who has ever walked away from me. My trust has been restored, and I no longer loosely use the word "friend." My expectations of friendship did not align with what God says. He did exceedingly, abundantly, above all I could have ever imagined or even hoped for. God gifted me with some beautiful sisters who I know love me, and I love them. These women pray for me, challenge me, and push me to grow deeper in God. I no longer have to tread on thin ice, worrying if I would be abandoned again. These chosen few do not have a problem holding me accountable, and I experience many God-encounters when in their presence. We can agree to disagree and still respect each other in our prospective places. Then, we can get ice cream! Our relationships are built on the foundation of Christ, and prayer is our daily diet.

Refining causes you to look at the things that once were and take a greater look at what remains. Thus, I am reminded of Hebrews 12:27 when Paul warns us that everything that can be shaken, will be, so the things that cannot be shaken shall remain. Although I experienced much shaking, I take refuge in knowing that Christ is interceding for me daily.

Jesus is praying for us daily. Once I got a revelation of what this really meant, I understood why He warned Peter about Satan. Jesus alerted Peter to Satan's plan in Luke 22:31. Satan had a desire to sift Peter's faith. That is still Satan's agenda today. He sifted several of my past relationships. *But!* Jesus said, *"I have prayed for you that your faith does not fail."* This is my hope dose.

The enemy wants to violently shake us so that our faith will be sifted. But God has given us power and authority! If we are not operating in that power, it is our fault. God has equipped us with every tool we need to accomplish every assignment and every relationship given to us. Just like a power socket, if a prong is not all the way pushed into it, no power will flow out of it. It's the same with us. Jesus is our power source. We need a direct connection to Him to be indued with His power.

Finally, God is an everlasting friend. Although I did not know this many years ago, I certainly do today. Proverbs 18:24 says, *"A man who has friends must himself be friendly, But there is a friend who sticks closer than a brother."* This journey has produced a greater relationship with Christ. My faith is intact and, now, I can strengthen others.

RECROWNING & Reflection

1. Would you have been able to forgive your best friend after betrayal?

   _____

   _____

   _____

   _____

   _____

2. How would you manage to stay at a church after being hurt by a member?

   _____

   _____

   _____

   _____

   _____

3. What is your understanding of being refined?

_____

_____

_____

_____

_____

4. In what areas has God restored you?

_____

_____

_____

_____

_____

ABOUT THE AUTHOR

Dr. Teresa Moore

As a community agent of change, radio co-host, minister and mental health professional, Dr. Moore lives a lifestyle of sowing seeds of hope and love. She is the owner and operator of Emages Counseling and Advocacy Services, where she offers a variety of therapeutic services, including but not limited to individual, married and group counseling; assessments; and educational treatment services to clients and families in the time of crisis. She has experience serving the developmentally disabled and mentally challenged population in various leadership roles. Holding multiple degrees in Religious Education, Counseling and Human Services she is known for masterfully combining the Word of God with psychological processes and procedures to help her clients break free from past wounds and hurts that continue to hold them hostage.

Dr. Moore uses a connective instructional style called "Living Life with your Hands Wide Open." Serving in multiple capacities of help and customer service, she seeks to go above and beyond the normal call of duty—and encourages clients, students and colleagues to do the same. Dr. Moore pinned her first book "Awaken to Win" April 2020. This book is filled with daily affirmations and prayer that is sure to jumpstart the day. She is a co-author in seven anthologies where she shares how God turned her mess into her message for His Glory. Affiliated with numerous professional and community organizations. Dr. Moore is sure to bring life to any dead situation she encounters. Dr. Moore is the wife of Fredrick Moore, and they are the parents of Cierra Crudup.

The Perverted Crown

Kimberly Hicks

I'm a 44-year-old divorced mother of four. In February of 2023, I went through deliverance. Deliverance takes place when a person receives prayer to remove unclean spirits from them. The New Testament of the Bible has many stories of Jesus and His disciples casting out unclean spirits. The problem today is that many believers think that, once you give your life to Christ, deliverance is no longer necessary.

That's the furthest thing from the truth.

Deliverance didn't end when Jesus died on the cross. Depending on what is happening in your life, some deliverance ministers are able to identify exactly which unclean spirits are in operation to cast them out by name in the name of Jesus. The following are some examples of spirits by name: the spirit of lust, the spirit of confusion, and the spirit of anxiety. This is why it is good to do an in-depth interview with the person who needs deliverance. If the deliverance minister is unable to identify the spirit by name, they will command the "unclean spirit" to leave in Jesus' name, without specifying a specific name for the spirit itself. Depending on how many spirits there are, deliverance could take minutes, hours, or even a series of deliverance sessions to set someone free. Deliverance, to me, is the ultimate form of healing.

But the person has to be willing to go through the process.

I was born in 1979 to a young mother and father. Both my parents saw abuse and unhealthy relationships growing up. As a young child, I witnessed multiple episodes of abuse, drug use and infidelity. Yes, I literally *witnessed* sexual infidelity. I also witnessed someone almost lose their life with a knife to their heart. I'd seen my fair share of dysfunctional relationships long before I was an adult.

One night, I was left in the care of a loved one. Little did I know, this was the night that would change the course of my life. This loved one was likely under the influence of drugs, alcohol or both. He decided this would be the night he would violate me. I was in bed sleeping when he touched my body and put his hand in my underwear. Before I knew it, he was masturbating next to me. He ejaculated *on* my vagina instead of *in* my vagina. He did me a favor by not penetrating me. But, nonetheless, the damage was done.

He gave me a towel to wipe myself, go back to sleep, and forget that it ever happened.

I don't remember if I was instructed not to say anything, but I didn't. If you've ever spoken with a person who was molested, most will tell you that they kept it to themselves for years. That's the intent of the spirit in operation. Once the victims are silenced, the spirit can continue to operate from generation to generation.

When I was in kindergarten, I remember being reprimanded for speaking foul sexual language. School administrators and teachers called my mother often to discuss my behavior, but she still had no idea what seed had been planted.

By the time I was twelve, one day, my mother came upstairs to my room and sat on the floor. She asked me, "Has anything ever happened to you? Has anyone touched you sexually?"

I answered softly, "Yes." I told her who it was when it happened and what happened. I knew this instantly crushed her. My mother has the gift of dreaming. God reveals things to her in dreams. This started when she was a young child. She had a dream about her father being killed and all the details surrounding it. This time, God had already revealed to her in a dream that something had indeed happened to me.

At the time, I didn't receive any type of therapy. I'm sure this was a matter my mother simply cried out to God about. Life progressed for me like the average teenager—or at least it seemed that way. I had my first consensual sexual encounter at the age of fifteen. I liked a guy who was two years older than me. I skipped a couple of my morning classes, we went to a house, and had sex. I really just wanted to get it over with for the sake of no longer being a virgin.

By the time I turned seventeen, I was pregnant with my first child. I aborted that pregnancy in the first trimester. That bothered me for years. I really didn't want to do it, nor was I in a position to care for another human. By the age of eighteen, I had collected four sexual partners. By the following year, I'd been hospitalized with the gift of an STD from my cheating boyfriend. Just imagine how embarrassed I was when I had to tell my mother I was in the hospital because of my current boyfriend. By the time I turned twenty, I'd collected more sexual partners and two more pregnancies. One of those pregnancies was from the same boyfriend who sent me to the hospital, but I miscarried in my first trimester. My third pregnancy was between two men I was dating at that time. I had no clue who had fathered my child, so I told them both they were the father. I had another miscarriage and, shortly after, the relationships with both men came to an end.

I had my first child at twenty-one with a man I didn't have a long history with. I spent most of my twenties partying, drinking, and enduring multiple failed relationships. In between the drinking, partying and men, I managed to finish school as an LPN. I maintained a 3.0 grade average throughout school. Suddenly, I was making really good money to party and drink. Unknowingly, as I collected more men, I was also collecting their demons and unclean spirits to add to my own.

My second child was born just after my twenty-ninth birthday. This was the pregnancy that slowed me down. Her father moved in with me and, during this time, I developed an emotional connection with sex. Prior to this, there were no emotional attachments to sex. Oftentimes, I had to drink to participate. Before my second daughter turned one, I was pregnant with my third child. I was still unmarried, unhappy, but pregnant. Shortly after my son was born (my third child), I got married. This marriage was not ideal, but I just wanted to be *married*. Four years later, I found myself pregnant with my fourth child and waiting for my divorce to be finalized, which couldn't happen until I gave birth.

After my divorce, I continued to have multiple failed relationships. In October 2021, I started dating someone with whom I thought I fell in love. He was different from all the other men I'd dated. He cared, he was attentive, and he was kind and gentle with me. However, in January of 2022, I received a personal prophecy. The prophecy was that one of my mother's daughters was about to get married. My youngest sister was already married, and my other sister wasn't dating anyone. I, therefore, assumed this prophecy was for little ole me. Not only did I accept this prophecy as my own, but that same night while I was hanging with my significant other, he said, "You are gonna be my future wife." I watched that video a hundred million times. This video served as my confirmation that the prophecy was in fact for me.

By April of 2022, it was over with the guy I thought I would once marry. This didn't go well for me. I found myself without an appetite and slowly losing weight. I can't remember this ever happening in the past. I held on to that prophecy until May of 2023. This "break up" hurt so bad, not to mention that everything else around me seemed like it was crumbling. I lost a job, which was 50% of my income. My business slowed down tremendously, and my children were acting out. Life was life-ing like it hadn't life-ed before. I needed something to relieve this pain. I knew it couldn't be alcohol and, for sure, it couldn't be drugs. I knew that leaning on a substance would lead to an addiction.

So, I ran to God. He welcomed me back with open arms.

Before I was freed from this idea, I was depressed. I lost weight. I had no desire to date or even hang out. I had no desire to be around anyone other than my close loved ones. There were times me and this guy would communicate fine. Other times, we fell out. During the fall outs, I had episodes of panic attacks. My body got extremely hot, tears ran down my face, and my heart raced uncontrollably. One day, I contemplated checking myself into a hospital. But how could I explain this to my family? That was another day I spent on the floor in tears. During this time, I cried more than I ever have in my entire life.

He would block me, then unblock me. A couple of times, I asked about us dating again. He simply wasn't interested. Now, Kim prior to 2021 would have blocked him and been on to the next man. Because of this prophecy though, I just could not let this idea go. I just couldn't let this man go. It didn't help that the YouTube algorithm kept sending me videos about kingdom spouses and prodigal spouses. This community of women were in bondage just as I was. They've been waiting years on a man they believe is their husband. I fell into that group of women. What a painful experience that was. That is just another tactic of the enemy to delay our promise of marriage.

If you ever receive a prophecy, before coming into agreement with it, always pray and ask God if this was a word from Him and what should you do next. If this was not a word from God, immediately divorce those words, renounce them, and come out of agreement with them. Your prayer should be, "Father, if this word was from you, I come in agreement with it and I need your guidance on what I am to do next. If this word was not from you, I rebuke those words immediately. I renounce and divorce those words spoken to and about me. May those words fall to the ground and bear no fruit in my life, in the mighty name of Jesus."

Remember that the devil doesn't create a thing. Therefore, he perverts the things of God, including prophecy.

In May of 2022, I started fasting consistently, in hopes that this relationship could be saved. This guy only pushed me further away. Yet, I still received "demonic confirmations." In June of 2022, I started working on my brand, Refurbished Souls. I started this business in 2019 to help women heal from emotional trauma. This business didn't last past 2019 because I gave up on it. I gave up on it because of a guy I was dating. I found out he was in a long-term relationship. That was disappointing, to say the least.

I blamed God for letting that happen. I spent a couple of months mad at God. Can you believe I was mad at God for a choice I made without consulting Him? *How could I help someone else, and I couldn't even help myself?* I have since repented. In my pain, I started the Refurbished Souls Facebook group and planned the first of many summits called Matters of the Heart.

By this time, I had run across a community of women who believed God told them a certain person was their husband. Now, this put false hope in my heart, which gave me the fuel to keep believing this man was my future husband. I continued to fast, pray and draw closer to God. In August of 2022, I was introduced to the ministry of Tiphani Montgomery. That woman inspired me to dig deeper into the Word of God. While watching one of her videos, I was introduced to Pastor Kevin L. A. Ewing from The Bahamas. This man has the gift of teaching. He broke the Bible down in such a way that I hungered to learn more about God's Word.

Coming off another fast in October of 2022, Pastor Ewing posted a video called "The Competing Spiritual Spouse." What he described in this video was what I had been experiencing most of my life. He explained how this spiritual spouse was an unclean spirit, which had oppressed individuals until it is cast out. Although the term "spiritual spouse" is not biblical, unclean spirits are. Now I know why my life took the turn it did. That unclean spirit had legal rights to my life from the acts of sex. Even though it was not consensual, it was still sex. Sex is a sin when you are not married, no matter what age you are.

For every time I had sex as an unmarried woman, I'm pretty sure I collected more unclean spirits. Until now, I didn't understand why I was having sex in my dreams and would literally have an orgasm in real life. Those orgasms always woke me up. One thing I realized was this never happened when anyone else was around. Dreams of having sex, unexplainable body odor (no doctors could find the cause), and many failed relationships were some of the characteristics of the "spiritual spouse." I encourage you to watch his video for a more detailed explanation.

He instructed anyone dealing with this to always rebuke and denounce this act once we were awake. I started doing this and, ironically, the dreams came more frequently! They used to be every couple of months. Now, they were coming every couple of weeks. I grew tired. At times, I didn't pray after the dreams. One common thing about those dreams was that I could never see the person's face. It was like a "white out" appearance.

I still was determined to be freed of this thing. I kept feeding my spirit the Word of God. I kept fasting, and I was led to another video. This was posted by two sisters who have a YouTube page called "Soft Lift Through Christ." The video spoke about one sister and how she went through deliverance.

I then knew that's what I needed. I reached out to my mother because I knew she had a friend who has a deliverance ministry. I planned to go ASAP, but there was a snowstorm and service was canceled. That following week, I attended my first deliverance session. I did three sessions overall and the dreams stopped. The odor left. I knew, without a doubt, that this unclean spirit was real and now gone.

At this point, unfortunately, I was still believing this man was my husband. We spoke occasionally, but in no way were we dating or working on a future relationship together. I wasted many days with this man on my mind. It was absolute torment. Because I have an iPhone, when you swipe right to the last screen, it shows picture memories. Well, one day I swiped to the last screen on the right, and, at the top of screen, it said text *****. My phone has never done that before and has not done it since then. Many times, I felt like I was receiving confirmation that we were supposed to be married. I now know these were "demonic confirmations." Remember that the enemy is perverts the things of God. These confirmations were sent to keep me bound, to keep me believing in something that was not of God. There was a time I thought I heard God about this situation, but that was still the acts of that "unclean spirit."

In my disobedience, we had our last sexual encounter. This time, I felt used. I'd never felt that way with him before.

This happened after I received deliverance. A couple of days went by, and I asked him, "Why is it that our time together is so far and few in between?"

His response was just what I needed to fuel my next fast. He said, "I'm not going to start something I'm not ready to commit to."

That was it. I was done, but I needed help to officially let go.

There was a fast coming up, but I debated if I wanted to participate. It was for twenty-five days; however, I committed to it.

I decided to fast for twenty-five days. The fast was from 6 a.m. to 3 p.m. daily. Instead of eating, I was praying and reading the Bible. The first couple of days, I cried a lot. Slowly, I could feel myself becoming free from this idea of marriage to this man who ultimately had moved on. Before the fast ended, I was free. God had once again delivered me. I made a video to share on Facebook about what I did for closure. Shortly after I posted the video, I received a message from this same man saying his "goodbyes" right before he blocked me. In that moment, I turned on my praise music and worshipped God. This was my confirmation that the enemy was *defeated*. In the past, these types of messages from him would cause me to break down, at times crying uncontrollably.

I had to pray that God would help me forgive this man. It's not that he misled me or even lied to me. I still had to make sure there weren't any remnants of unforgiveness in my heart. He was just a vessel the enemy used to delay me from what God really has for me. The enemy wanted me to believe God lied to me, but God doesn't lie. His plan was to drive me crazy, get me to turn on God, and ultimately never see the promises of God. Boy was that liar wrong! What he did was pushed me back to God. The pain was so unbearable. This was a pain only God could fix. So, I fled to the restorer, the healer, Jesus Christ.

Romans 8:28 says, *All things work together for those that love the Lord and are called according to His purpose.* Do you see how this worked out? He sent this man to destroy me, but I ended up back in the will of the Lord.

Another win for the Kingdom!

Something that brought me great pain also led me back to Christ. While trying to keep my mind occupied through it all, I had my first summit. These summits have brought healing to many women and also brought healing to me in the process. Lord willing, the summits will continue every three months, even expanding to other nations.

Refurbished Souls, to date, has hosted four summits, with number five in the planning stages. The Facebook group has approximately nine hundred members so far. Every first

Wednesday of the month, we fast as a group. That was something God put on my heart toward the end of 2022. I pray fasting will become a regular part of our group. Fasting is not easy. But once you see the fruit of your sacrifice, you will want to incorporate fasting into your walk with Christ.

With each fast, I feel like God was giving me the pieces to the puzzle to my life. Although my puzzle isn't complete, it's almost finished. I expected that I would get direct answers to my prayers, but it didn't go that way. You know how the saying goes, "If you give them too much too soon, they won't appreciate it." Through this all, God was building my prayer life, my worship life, and my faith. He was developing my godly character so I can walk in the purpose He planned for me before the foundation of this earth. What general would send their warriors to battle without first preparing them?

No matter what you've done or how bad you're feeling, we serve a God who welcomes us back with open arms. He forgets the things of our past, so must we. His Word says that this kind only comes out by praying and fasting. That means when you prayed and cried, cried and prayed, it's time to fast. Fasting, by biblical definition, means not eating. You will have to make the sacrifice of not eating to crucify your flesh. It may not all come in one prayer or one fast, but it will come. Matthew 6:33 says, *Seek ye the Kingdom of*

God and His righteousness and all these things will be added to you. Psalm 84:11 says, *No good thing will He withhold from the one who walks uprightly.* To see every promise of God for your life, you have to seek Him and be obedient.

RECROWNING *& Reflection*

1. What's that thing in your life that, no matter how hard you've tried, no matter how much you've prayed, it wouldn't budge?

_____

_____

_____

_____

_____

2. What does being healed look like for you?

_____

_____

_____

_____

_____

3. What would you do if I told you that your healing could be simply tied to your obedience to God's Word?

_____

_____

_____

_____

_____

4. How should you respond to a prophecy you receive?

_____

_____

_____

_____

_____

5. How can you make fasting a regular part of your life?

_____

_____

_____

_____

_____

ABOUT THE AUTHOR

Kimberly Hicks

$\mathcal{W}$ith a mission to educate and empower women, Kimberly Hicks established her company for passionate and ambitious women to share her expertise with the community. As a 44-year-old mother of four, Kimberly has a lot of love and passion to share her knowledge, as well as dedicating time and effort for a positive impact on the community at large. She has a purposely driven goal to bring up and inspire women from all around the globe.

With over 20 years of offering hope, daily communication with patients, and making a big difference in peoples' lives as a nurse, her passion for more positive impact led her to pursue her dream to reach more individuals. In hope, she brings other women up, helping them get to the perfect version of themselves. Believing wholeheartedly that women deserve to have a consistent source of positive energy, educational content, as well as inspiration, Kimberly works

together with others around the globe to take strategic
action and drive change for women's empowerment.

Uncrowned

Dominique Cryor

As a young girl, I always envisioned myself as a wife, mom and businesswoman that was super successful in my career, happy in my personal life, and far removed from the trauma of my past. I always thought that if I could just get away from the hurt, the pain and the rejection that I felt, in some way, my life would magically evolve into this fairytale existence. Well, that surely was not the case for me at that current point in my life. I was 32 years old, with four young children. I was swimming in debt. I was the only one working, managing the household, and being the daily Uber driver for everyone's appointments, except my own. I did this all while being mentally, emotionally and physically exhausted from ten years of marriage to a man whom I, at one point, believed to be "the one."

I spent most of my youth and early adulthood trying to figure out who was, never really completely grasping the totality of me. I was rejected at conception by parents who were teenagers. They had no clue what they wanted or what they would do with a baby. Only for that cycle to continue as a growing child, I was abandoned my biological father and was never able to forge a relationship. That left me broken in a way that was hard for me to even verbalize. So, I did what so many other rejected people do: I became everything for everyone else. I learned to do my best to please those around me so they would accept me. Because of how God created me, I never was able to go along with wrong for long.

I eventually grew to become a defensive, hard, take-no-crap, fight whomever to protect me and mines type of woman. I ended up marrying my high school sweetheart, who I know and understand was a mirror image of myself. He was rejected by family, abused by parents, left on his own to figure out this thing called life. It left him broken in places beyond repair. So, because two broken people, who had no idea what brokenness was or looked like, stayed together, we reproduced it together. To my surprise, there was so much more under the surface that I didn't know or understand. Over time, I learned that a broken soul is hard to be mended without Jesus' power, strength, deliverance and love.

I spent the majority of my first marriage covering for my then husband's many outbursts of anger in front of our children, family and friends. I excused them and turned a blind eye to the infidelity, mentally blocking out the late-night calls, hiding the bruises on my body, and pain in front of others—all while attempting to keep a straight face to sell my kids pipe dreams that it would get better eventually. I wanted them to believe the abuse they saw weekly, or sometimes daily, would be fine. We would work it out and get through it.

One night, I was arguing and fighting with my then husband and our kids ran upstairs. To my surprise, when I went up to find them, they were hiding in the closet, crying. In that moment, after all the times before, and all the fights, somehow, at this moment, my eyes were literally opened. I knew that my life was in shambles. I needed to get out of this toxic relationship. In my ignorance, I thought it would be easy, but it would take me years to get out. I'm sure that many people would say, "That's the moment you realized it was toxic?" Yes, because in my warped mind, I was doing all this for my kids and husband. I was sacrificing myself, my happiness, my self-respect, my peace, for my family. I thought that if I stayed, I was somehow proving my loyalty and love. I believed in my heart that I could somehow change this man and, at some point, that he would see my sacrifices and grow.

I never wanted my children to know the pain that I had endured coming from a dysfunctional home with divorced parents. I never wanted them to experience the great sense of helplessness that divorce brought to families. I'm sure like so many other women and men that grew up in traumatic environments that have children, we often relive our experiences in our minds. We vow that our children won't experience those same hurts. But somehow, we find ourselves in the very situation we despised.

After all the years of me trying to understand, and waiting for this man child to grow up and become the person that I imagined him to be, I had to face a hard truth that it was never going to happen. I vividly recall the day that all the years of arguments, abuse, gaslighting and manipulation came into the clearest view of my life. I received an email from my then husband's doctor's office. As I sat in my truck, reading over the details of every test performed and typical responses of patients that have these types of tests performed, I was stunned. I felt like my stomach was in my toes. I was completely numb and devastated. I read and reread the results. They were conclusive that he was diagnosed with multiple mental disorders, several of which I knew to be true because of all the things I'd experienced for years. The symptoms lined up. The behavior manifest ions lined up. The personality changes and other personality symptoms lined up. The gaslighting, the overtalking, the mental punishments I endured all lined up. I literally sat there in my truck, completely silent for a very long while, attempting to process all the information I read.

Even though I was upset about the diagnosis, all those years, I knew something was wrong. However, I never trusted my own gut enough to believe what I saw in front of me. I thought about my children simultaneously. I was terrified for them. What would happen to them as they got older, and their father never got any better? Although this new information was a lot to take in, I was relieved because of what I felt down in my heart. All those years, I thought it was something wrong with me.

Now, I'm not a person who only likes to see the horrible parts of others and not look at my own self. Of course, because we had been in an on-and-off relationship since I was fifteen, I had to take some responsibility for the fact that I chose to stay and marry him at twenty-two years old. Was I a perfect wife? Absolutely not because no individual on the planet is perfect. Yes, I had days, as well, when I was overwhelmed by my small children, or I was working tons to support the household so much that I lashed out. But I never deserved the treatment that I got in return.

Now, with this diagnosis, things shifted even more within my household. I had made the decision that I wouldn't tell my children. They wouldn't know what or how to interpret the information, so I hid it from them. When their father would have his outbursts, or we would fight, I tried to find ways to explain things. But it never came across well. Although I had been going through hell all this time, I believed in my heart that now that we knew what the problem was, we could fix it together. I looked up treatment options and doctors who could help. I even told very close family so they, too, could help me "heal this diagnosis." But it seemed that all my efforts to help make things better only created more turmoil and no resolution.

The arguments got worse. The physical abuse got worse. Cursing me out in front of the kids got worse. The personality changes got worse. The manipulation of others got worse, so much so that when I finally told someone about the abuse, no one believed me. There were so many nights that I lied out on the floor and prayed that God would either heal him and fix the marriage or help me to do more so that he would know that I had his back. I was going to be as loyal as I could be to him through this time so we could move forward. On one occasion, someone asked me, "What are you doing to upset him?" To my shock, I literally started crying. I hung up the phone. I called another individual who is literally family. I knew for sure this person would help me, considering that we had a very close relationship.

When I called and verbalized the situation, the response I received shook me to my core and broke my heart at the same time. I was told, "That's not my responsibility! He's your husband, not mine! So, what do you want me to do?!" I remember looking at my cell phone, completely confused and baffled at what I'd just heard and hung up. At that moment, I decided in my own mind and heart that I was going to be completely done with everyone and everything. I was going to focus on me, my children and our safety.

Over the course of a year, I continued to experience various types of abuse—all while attempting to save money, manage my household, be at all the kids' recitals, band assembles, and everything in between. Because the behaviors got worse, so did the punishments and delusions. My ex-husband would curse me out in front of the boys and sometimes attack me physically, then not speak to me for days. He also told my boys that I was being mean to him and that I hated him and our family. One particular time, on our youngest son's birthday, he kidnapped him, his siblings and friend for hours. He told everyone that I was crazy and that I was trying to kill him—all because I was taking them to play at an indoor trampoline park and he didn't want to celebrate our son's birthday at all.

Living with a spouse who is mentally ill is one of the hardest battles any person can face. I don't believe up until this point in my life that I had faced that type of evil or hell before. I feel like I was living in a house with the floors packed and overflowing with eggshells. I didn't want to make the wrong move. It was sometimes impossible for me to keep my own sanity. It felt chaotic at times. The feelings of loneliness, shame, pity, rejection and self-rejection were horrific, on top of all the other names he called me on a regular basis. Because I never, ever made myself a priority, I never understood my value. I thought if I served everyone with everything I had, that would somehow fill the giant hole in my soul, and I would be made whole. In my mind, deciding to leave and putting myself first was one of the hardest parts. I went back and forth with myself.

What would other people say if I just up and left my mentally ill husband? How would members of the church look at me? How would God feel about me after making that type of decision? I thought about my sons and my daughter. What would they think? Would they still love me if I decided to choose myself, even over them, because of all the hell I was enduring? I'm sure that there have been many people who have been, or are going through, a similar experience. I'm here to let you know that it's 100 percent fine for you to choose peace, love, God and balance.

In 2019, I filed for divorce. I felt the peace of God when I did, but a new challenge arose. The Lord had to take me on another journey. It was called healing and wholeness. Jeremiah 31:28 speaks about how the Lord watched over the afflictions, breakdowns and destruction. But then it says how He will build and plant. Unfortunately, in our judgmental culture, everyone tells you what they think and how to move past a situation. Folks can say, "Oh you deserve better than this or that!" But they don't tell you how to heal your mental health after being in relationship with a mentally ill individual. I found myself turning and looking for a blueprint from other women, or even men, who talked about how to mend the broken places in the mind. However, I didn't find one, So, God made me one.

I want to say this to everyone who will read this that has experienced any similar issues. You are not crazy! Now this statement may be confusing to others, but those who experienced this level of trauma need to know that someone understands you. Having heard the very opposite for years made me question myself in every area of my life. I had to decide that I was not going to let this experience define me or my ability to have a healthy relationship one day.

One of the very first things that came up to me was to forgive myself. I had to forgive myself for staying all those years, knowing that deep down it was never going to get better. I had to forgive myself for being scared of everything that was related to me seeing, knowing and believing that I had value. The journey of forgiveness is the first stop on the road to freedom. Choose to forgive the other person and everyone involved. Yes, this will hurt and bring you to your knees in tears and groans. But it's necessary. Your ability to forgive yourself and others frees you from the hurt the experience created. It allows you to hold your head up high without shame or fear of the naysayers.

Secondly, I had to decide to heal the wounds of my past in order to have a healthy future. I decided to see a therapist, one who was God-filled and who could get to the root of the problem. This three-year long relationship that I developed was one of the greatest tools God allowed me to obtain. I used those times in the office to unpack me, my losses, my regrets, my hurts and rejection. I spent many of those days barely able to speak. Yet, as the tears rolled down my face, I felt freedom ll. I used the tools given to me in my daily life. The Bible says that faith without works is dead. So, I exercised it daily when I felt overwhelmed and dismayed.

Thirdly, I stopped making decisions for my life based upon the potential backlash that I thought or even knew my ex-husband would display. I decided to no longer consider his feelings, ideas and perspective on my life. It was no longer controlled by him. Being in a relationship with an individual whose mind is not regulated by them all the time will make you believe that every move you make without them, or their approval, is wrong in some way. I learned to consider no one but God and my children. The first few times that major decisions were made in my life after divorce were terrifying. I was expecting arguments and fights. But when I realized that the response wasn't coming, I felt free.

Lastly, I began the journey to discover *me*. Who was Dominique? What did I like about myself? What did I want to improve? I had dived into myself in a way that I never had before. To my surprise, I discovered dreams forgotten, gifts untapped, potential unknown and unmet. I found love for myself and God that I never knew could run so deeply. I learned to trust God in a brand-new way. I learned to love my children in a way that wasn't unhealthy for them or myself. I continued to choose to become who God spoke from the throne room of heaven. I chose God's image and plan for the next part of my life and received the freedom that I waited years for.

God doesn't bring evil into our lives. However, our choices and, sometimes the choices of others, can hinder us in ways that will take us off course for years. But God doesn't desire us to stay that way. I pray that if you're starting your healing journey, or you have been on the road of healing for a while, that you welcome the Almighty God into every place. Let His Word and presence saturate every place of pain, hurt, disappointment, and despair to be engulfed up by His great love for you. It's your time to, not only be healed, but to be made whole. Your time is now to be whole in your mind, emotions, and soul so the good plans, the God ideas, the God purposes, can flow to you and from you.

RECROWNING *& Reflection*

1. How has your past trauma affected your relationships? How do you plan to change behaviors and habits to create healthier relationships?

    _____

    _____

    _____

    _____

    _____

2. What action strategies do you plan to take to help you reach your goals?

    _____

    _____

    _____

    _____

    _____

3. How are you planning to build a stronger relationship and faith in God on your healing journey?

_____

_____

_____

_____

4. What do healthy boundaries look like on your journey of healing and wholeness? Are you afraid to place boundaries?

_____

_____

_____

_____

5. What dreams and goals did you place on the back burner that have never left your heart and mind?

_____

_____

_____

_____

ABOUT THE AUTHOR

Dominique Cryor

*D*ominique Cryor is a Detroit native, wife, mother of five, nurse by profession, published author, etiquette and professional development consultant, business owner, and a domestic and sexual abuse survivor. Dominique serves currently as Associate Pastor alongside her husband at Kingdom Now in Warren, MI.

Not a stranger to life's challenges, Dominique dealt with rejection and abandonment issues at a very young age that landed her life spiraling into cycles of dysfunction for many years of her adult life. At the age of nine, she was molested by a family member, which further enforced the rejection and despair that she felt. She had her first child at the age of eighteen and spent the remainder of her teenage years figuring out what to do with her life. However, partying and drinking became her way to numb the pain and hurt inside her heart.

At the age of twenty-two, she became pregnant with her second child and was unwed. Dominique feeling completely crushed, rededicated her life to Christ, on her living room floor in the middle of night. From that moment on, she decided that she wanted God's plan for her life above her own.

Dominique married young and thought somehow her love would help her now ex-husband heal from his own trauma and pain. Over the course of the ten years of marriage, she learned that her thinking was completely wrong. During the marriage, she had two more children and was deeply depressed. She dealt with verbal, emotional, financial and physical abuse for the majority of the marriage. She filed for divorce and chose to leave in an attempt to show her children that this is not how God designed marriage to be in His Word. In September of 2019, her ex-husband tried to take her life, holding her at gunpoint. After surviving this ordeal, Dominique's resolve to live out her purpose in Christ became stronger than ever. She knew that God's plan was not for her to die in the street, but to declare His great name to every nation.

In March of 2020, while working as a nurse during the pandemic, God gave her instructions to launch one of the businesses in her heart. Marie Decorum School of Protocol was birthed out, but now is known as Marie Decorum

Christian Etiquette School. This school is a place where students learn who they are through God's Word and how to conduct themselves in any and every situation and manner. Dominique has had the privilege to teach high school students and conduct her etiquette school annually.

Now that she has emerged fully refined and spiritually fortified, Dominique married again by God's amazing grace to the man of her dreams in October 2022. She's growing and continuing to become who God ordained her to be.

Dominique has a great passion for women to grow and walk in the fullness of who God says they are. Now fully healed and whole, Dominique blazes the trail, inspiring women daily to become whole in every way possible.

ABOUT

So It Is Written

We help entrepreneurs write the ONE book that will expand their reach and get them to SIX figures in record time! Period!

As the leading content curators for six-figure authorpreneurs and entrepreneurs, So It Is Written is best known for helping them package and leverage their expertise into a bestselling book, which amplifies their brand, accelerates their paydays and attracts bigger opportunities!

Let us help you brand in excellence as an author and entrepreneur so you can develop multiple streams of income from just ONE book!

Call us at 313-777-8607 today or email info@soitiswritten.net for more details about our services. We look forward to working with you to make your project one of excellence!

www.ingramcontent.com/pod-product-compliance
Lightning Source LLC
Chambersburg PA
CBHW060327130626
46553CB00003B/943